LET THE DIRT HAVE IT

A Backwoods Grimoire for the Soft and the Furious

TENDING THE YOU THAT SURVIVED
BOOK TWO

la tetra o.

This is a work of original authorship. While the content
may reflect spiritual or ritual traditions, this book is not
intended as clinical advice or as a substitute for
professional therapy or counseling.

Printed in the United States of America

First Edition
ISBN (paperback): 979-8-9994526-0-3
LCCN: 2025919509

Published by Ash + Anthology
What the fire didn't take, we tell.
Ashandanthology.com

For inquiries:
books@latetrao.com

DEDICATION

For the ones I come from.
The ones who knew how to bury things without
shovels.
The ones who grieved in kitchens, whispered to
dirt, and made it through without ever being
witnessed.

I saw you.
I stayed.

This is ours.

CONTENTS

Call this a table if you must, but it is altar. It is ash, it is dust. Here you may find the names of what you've carried, and maybe, the place to let it go.

The grave don't close right
when the truth's still
walkin' around.

THE INVITATION

You don't owe this text your softness.
You don't have to heal here.
You can walk in with your teeth clenched,
or not at all.

This is not a guide. Not a process. Not a gentle
hand on the shoulder telling you it's time to let go.
It's a burial ground and a place to name what never
got to rot properly.

Every page is a laying down.
A laying to rest. A laying to ruin.
Some entries are shaped like spells.
Others like secrets.

You'll find offerings you've made before and ones
you swore you never would.
There is no map. Just dirt, memory, and maybe
something waiting beneath them.

You don't need to relate.
You are not asked to agree.
This is not about common ground.
It's about holy ground.
The kind that shows up under your feet the
moment you stop pretending they don't hurt.

What you carry is yours.
What you keep is yours.
What you leave here?
That's between you and the dirt.

Enter only if you mean to.
Leave when you need to.

Nothing here is binding.
But something might finally loosen.

WHO IS THIS FOR?

This is for the ones who weren't given a grave for what was lost.

The ones who carry the dead like a second spine.
Who keep secrets in their stomachs and call it
"coping."
For the ones who didn't get closure – just silence.
Just forgetting.
Just an ache that kept reverberating long after the
quiet set in.
For the daughters of denial.
The sons of suspicion.
The ones who side-eye tenderness but crave it
anyway.
For those who learned to hold their breath because
screaming was too expensive.
Because grief had to be whispered.
Because rage made people leave.
This is for the ones who unlearn in the dark. Who
spit in the dirt and call it ceremony. Who
remembers what was done
even when no one said it out loud.
It's not for the polished.
Not for the ones who need step-by-step salvation.
A clean moral,
A happy ending.
This is for those who have buried it and still feel it
shifting below the earth.
If you've ever whispered what should've been
hollered...

This book is yours.

CONTENT NOTE

If you find yourself up in here, it's on purpose.

This body holds sharp things.
Inside these pages are stories, spells, and unsaid
truths that deal with:

- Sexual trauma and violation
- Grief and complicated mourning
- Food addiction and body betrayal
- Emotional manipulation and withheld care
- Anger that never got to be holy
- Pettiness, shame, and the sacred act of
  saying it anyway

Some of these Offerings are soft. Some are
venomous.
None of them come with a bow.
This is not a book about *healing*.
It's about what healing tried to outrun –
and what found you anyway.
It's a **grimoire** for the haunted and the honest – for
the ones who needed a place to bury it.

You made it here. That's no accident.

Mind how you carry what you find.

I HELD IT TOGETHER AND KEPT IT AT BAY AS I COULD. NOW IT'S GOT TEETH.

I AIN'T HERE TO HEAL YOU...

This ain't a warning. It's a word.

This ain't a book of closure.
This ain't a *guide* to letting go.
This ain't where I tell you to breathe through it and forgive.

This is where I spit the bones out. Where I name what tried to decay inside me. Where I bury the ghosts with their mouths still open.
Where I say what I couldn't say while it was still happening.

This ain't crafted.
It's dragged out the dirt, still bleeding.
Ain't stitched up or nothin'.
Just stopped leaking long enough to speak.

So if you're holding this, *you've already been marked.*

You may come to it as **judge, witness, or gravedigger.**

Or maybe to quietly bear witness.
As **practitioner or patient.**
Or perhaps a forensic auditor.
As a **victim or perpetrator.**
Or likely a shameless voyeur.

You might not know which one you are until the dirt starts to recognize you.

This book moves differently.

There are no lessons here.
No syllabus.
No long walk toward resolution.

Just this:
The title is a command.
Let the Dirt Have It.

Not tidy it. Not compost it. Not grow from it. Let it spoil. Let it reek. Let it be laid down.

It's a call to the parts of you still entertaining the thing that split you. The parts that know better and ache anyway.

It don't knock.
It don't beg.
It don't wait for you to be ready.

This is a truth that shows up muddy, loud, and unasked for.
And still – it's yours.

The chapters don't exist.
Only Offerings.
They are letters, spells, confessions, and names spoken into soil.

This is how they breathe.

The Spill is what poured out when the seal broke.

The Burial is the closing – a ritual, a curse, or a laying-down.

The Surrender is a private act,
witnessed but never instructed. (You don't follow it.
You just feel it.)

Some Offerings are tender. Some are venom. Some
ache. Some spit.

None carry the expectation of warm reception.

If you came looking for peace,
you might want to go find it somewhere else.

If you came looking for truth,
sit down and get your hands dirty.

A NOTE ON LANGUAGE

The words in this book are jagged on purpose.
They're not refined.
They're not balanced.
They weren't run through a strainer.

Some of them bite.
Some of them curse.
Some of them couldn't come out any other way but
hurried and ugly.

I'm not cleaning them up.

This grimoire don't speak in church voice.
It speaks in blood.
In breath.
In what finally came forced its way out after being
held in too long.
If that makes you uncomfortable…

Good.

A NOTE ON RITUAL AND RISK

Not every spell is meant to be cast.

Some are meant to be witnessed.
Some are meant to be buried.

This isn't a spellbook in the traditional sense, but
you might find yourself dabbling in these practices
anyway.

Some words in here look suspiciously like
instructions. Others open doors.

None are demands. All are testimonies.
What you choose to do with them is sacred and
yours.

Move with care.
With discernment.
With your own spirit as a compass. Let the dirt
guide you – but never command you.

You are sovereign. You are soil. You already know.

But understand this:
You've been invited to one woman's private
workings, made visible.

If you've never seen someone prepare for their own
freedom, this might confuse you. You may mistake
the gestures for performance.
The rituals for rules.

But these pages are not prescriptions. They are confessions, ceremonies, and grief songs meant to be *felt*, not *followed*.

Let your body say yes.
Let your lineage say no.
Let your own dirt decide
what belongs to you –
and what's meant to pass right on through.

THE NAMING

Offerings to What Was Done
but Never Spoken

COME CLEAN.
COME SHAKING.
COME WRONG.
THIS IS WHERE THE MOUTH
REMEMBERS
WHAT THEY MADE IT HOLD.
SAY IT.
OUT LOUD.
AND ALL THE WAY.

an offering to
the corpse that refused
to stay dead

For what kept rising even after
it was buried deep.

I gave it dirt,
and it still clawed its way back up.
Dressed in memory.
Talking like it never tried to kill me.

**This is for the ghost that
doesn't know it's gone.**

THE SPILL

I buried you clean.
Said the words.
Lit the candle.
Burned the pages.
Closed the chapter.

Ashes. Dust. Silence.

And still –
you crawl back.
Not loud. Just present.
In the tightness of my chest when I smell that smell.
In the way my body tenses at voices that sound too
sure.
In the laugh that dies in my throat when I realize
I'm being watched.

You never left.
You just went quiet.

And every time I start to feel free,
you lean on my peace like it's yours to collect.

You show up in my dreams with a new face.
You arrive in me again.
Same shape, same sting.
Show up in my throat, where the words stick.

You survived every ritual I built to forget you.
Every prayer.

Every spell.
Every silence.

I thought I was done.

But you –
you're the grief that changes outfits.
The pain that learns my new address.

You're the corpse with a calendar.
Always back when joy bears fruit,
breathing frost on the harvest.

I try to convince myself that I imagined you.

That I'm the cold one.
But I know your footprints.
And I'm tired of pretending I don't.

I don't want to keep planting joy in dirt you haven't
left.

You were real.
You hurt me.
And you don't get to rise again
every time I move forward
without looking over my shoulder.

This was your last resurrection.
The door is shut.
The ground is salted.
Nothing else grows here in your name.

THE BURIAL

I don't owe your ghost another witness.

I named you.
I grieved you.
I laid you down.

You weren't unfinished –
just unwilling.

But I'm done dragging the memory of you
through every season that tried to bless me.

I'm not waiting for you to stay buried.
I'm deciding that you are.

You don't get to haunt what you no longer hold.

THE SURRENDER

She didn't cry this time.
Didn't write a poem.
Didn't ask the ancestors for help.

She just walked barefoot to the back of the yard,
dug a hole with her hands,
and spat in it.

8

Not out of hate, but finality.
A salt line from her own mouth.
A seal the dead couldn't cross.

She dropped in the scrap of paper –
the last time she told the story.

Covered it with dirt.
Pressed it down with both palms.

Then stood and walked away without looking back.

Not because it didn't hurt –
but because this time,
she didn't confuse return with resurrection.

an offering to the moan they called mercy

For the body that begged sweet
just to survive it.

They thought I liked it.
Thought the sound meant stay.
But my body was just trying
not to break too loud.

**This is for the noise they
mistook for consent.**

THE SPILL

I didn't say yes.
However, my body did something that indicated *it*
had.

That's what haunts me.

Not the act.
Not the intention.
Not even the violation.

It was the moan.

The way it slipped out like it belonged to
someone else.
The way it saved me.

Because it did.
Didn't it?

It kept the room quiet.
It made it go faster.
It made them think I was... *with it.*

And I've hated myself for that sound ever
since.
Because it wasn't pleasure. It was protocol.
A ritual of release I learned without ever being
taught.
If I moan, it ends quicker.
If I moan, I stay alive.

If I moan, I get to keep my body in one piece,
even if I leave it behind.

They called it mercy.
They said I leaned into it.
Said I was "responsive."
Said I was "sweet."

But that sound wasn't mine.
It was a costume.
It was a door I opened so I wouldn't be
ripped through.

You want to know what betrayal is?

It's your own throat vetoing your silence.

It's your own hips tilting, like they're grateful.
It's your body trying to survive in a way that
looks like seduction.

I wanted to scream.
But I swallowed it.
And the moan came out instead.

And for years, I've held funerals for that moment.

For years, I've tried to bury that moment –
but the sound wouldn't stay down.
It came back quiet, but certain, and made a home of
me.

What was meant to die nested.

And sometimes now, even when I'm touched
with love, that moan rises first.

Before the trust.
Before the breath.
Before the yes.

Like it's still waiting to be useful.
Still waiting to protect me.

But I don't need it anymore.
I want it out of me.
I want to slide it back
into the mouth of that hot summer afternoon
it was born in.

I want to unlearn it.
Unname it.
Reearth it.

THE BURIAL

I rebuke the sound that smothered my silence.
I rebuke the reflex they called relenting.
I rebuke the moan that bartered my body for safety.

You are not refuge. You are an instigator.
And I no longer want to carry you just in case.
Leave me.
Leave my throat to song, not silence.
Leave my *no* without fingerprints.
Leave my yes out your mouth.
Go back to the mouth that demanded you.
And die *there*.

14

THE SURRENDER

She sat still.
No candles. No chants. No tools.
Just nothingness so sharp it screamed.

She pressed two fingers to her throat,
right where the sound used to crawl up –
and hummed.

Not beautifully. Not melodically.
Just enough to remind her body what her
voice felt like when it wasn't a trick.
When it wasn't bait.
When it wasn't a plea in disguise.

She didn't speak.
Not for an hour. Not for a day.
She let her voice rest.

Not because it was tired –
but because it had been used without consent.
And when the silence returned,
it didn't mock her.
It bowed.

an offering to the smile that hid the exit

For the charm that kept me captive.

It opened every door –
except the one I needed.
I wore it like armor,
but it locked me in the room.

**This is for the sweetness that
silenced your scream.**

THE SPILL

You weren't joy.
You were strategy.

A flash of bone to prove I was fine.
A lift in the corner of my mouth so no one
would ask.
You were armor disguised as warmth.

And you worked.
God, you worked.

You got me through dinners where my hands
trembled under the table.
Through meetings where I wanted to scream.
Through bedrooms I never should've entered,
and didn't know how to leave.

You were my charm.
My access pass.
My shield.

You lingered like a hem I never unstitched.

And once I smiled,
they believed me.
Believed the version you made.
Lip gloss over a howl.
Charm with iron hinges.
A cage they called composure.

She's okay.
She's confident.
She's not scared.
She'll do it gladly.

They never saw the fracture.
Because of you, I learned how to endure
anything – as long as I could make it look good.
Sexy.
Easy.

But the price?

I forgot how to know when I was okay.
You corked my throat with a dimple.
Covered the sting with a joke.
Lingered like a hem I never unstitched.

And now…

Even when I want to cry,
I catch you trying to rise.
You were never the villain.
Just the filter.
The pretty lie.
The gate that made silence look polite.

And I played your prisoner willingly.
I chose their ease over my exit.

THE BURIAL

I release the performance that protected me.
I no longer dress danger in dimples.
That smile can stay behind.
It was never mine to carry.
I'm leaving with *my whole face.*

THE SURRENDER

She stood in the mirror, mouth closed
Not frowning.
Just true.
Then she smiled – not for joy, not for photo,
but to watch the mask form.
And when she saw it –
the practiced lift, the betrayal –
she touched it like a bruise.
Pressed her thumb to the place where the
betrayal always starts.
She didn't fix her face on the way out.
She let it twitch. Let it drop. Let it be hers.
Hard.
Like she was wiping away
done-too-good makeup.
Then she said it.
Low. Direct. Final.
"Fuck you."

And left the mirror fogged with her breath.
Uncleared.
A witness.
A refusal.
A closing door.

an offering to the habit that wears their face

For the pattern I kept calling a person.

It knocks like it's someone new.
Smiles with borrowed teeth.
Smells like hope but tastes like history.
I let it in again.

**This is for what you knew –
and did anyway.**

THE SPILL

I don't miss you.
I miss the rhythm.
The ritual.
The way you'd break me open just enough to feel
something –
but never enough to make it matter.

You became a pulse.
A cycle.
A spell I cast with muscle memory instead of magic.

I didn't come back for you.
I came back for the throbbing.

Because the throbbing was familiar.
Your chaos had routine.
Your silence had shape.
Your presence, a pattern.

You were a habit –
not a home.

And I kept relapsing.
Not because I believed you'd change.

But because I didn't want to change alone.

I knew what you were.
Knew what it cost.
But the craving wore your face.

And the face wore my name.

You made me forget that peace isn't boring.
That love doesn't need a cliff to prove it's real.
That adrenaline isn't intimacy.
That being chosen isn't the same as being cherished.

And now –
even when I know better –
my body still twitches toward your shadow.
Still mistakes emptiness for invitation.
Still aches for pain when it doesn't know what else
to feel.

I'm not in love with you.
I'm addicted to the version of me that survived you.

And I'm done rehearsing my own ruin.

THE BURIAL

I do not need pain to prove I'm living.
I do not need their face to remember my name.

I bury the pattern that wore their name.

Let the dirt harden.
Let the pattern stop breathing.
Let it wither.
Not where it wants to, but where I say.

THE SURRENDER

She took the jar to the back edge of the yard.
Her own private woods –
where the dirt stays cold long after winter ends.
Where nothing grows without permission.

Then she sealed it.
Wrapped it in black cloth.
Not to hide it, but to mark it as uninvited.

She buried it under the frostline,
where worms sleep and old roots forget their
names.

No prayer.
No thaw.
Just frozen ground and the silence that meant:

you don't get to rise again.

an offering to the clock that stole from me

For the hours that it took without asking.

It ticked through the grief
like it didn't notice.
Measured my healing with deadlines.
Called me lazy when I needed to stop.

**This is for the time you didn't
get to spend – and the
stillness it tried to shame.**

THE SPILL

You didn't tick.
You took.

Told me I was late before I even arrived.
Said I was behind –
behind her, behind him, behind schedule.
Behind the version of me who started sooner.

You never asked why I froze.
Why I stalled.
Why I stayed in survival mode ten harvests deep.

You held me down, peeled my lids back,
made me watch while others bloomed
without bleeding first.

You just kept counting.
Laughing.
Mocking.

You turned growth into shame.
Turned "not yet" into failure.
And I put my trust in you.

I rushed what needed ripening.
Cut myself open before I was even picked.
Said yes when I already had language for no.
Tried to tend my garden
with a looking glass in one hand
and a brass witness in the other.

I kept chasing the girl who lived without my grief.
But the truth is –
I lost time.
Not to laziness.
Not to lack.

To mourning.
To vigilance.
To caretaking.
To betrayal.

To people I loved
who couldn't love me without taking pieces.

I. Lost. Time.
And I'm done being sorry for it.

You will not shame me for starting late
when I was busy saving myself from disappearing.
You will not measure my worth
in milestones I never asked for.
You will not make urgency my master.

I'm not behind.
I'm here.

And that is its own miracle.

THE BURIAL

I break covenant with the clock.
I am not late.
I am mine.

THE SURRENDER

She didn't wind the watch.
Didn't set the time.
Didn't ask the sun where she should be.
She dropped the timepiece into
a bowl of saltwater
and watched it drown slow,
then pressed the rusted thing into the soil,
time undone, and planted.

an offering to the one
who loved me safely
from afar

For the tenderness that never got
close enough to touch.

They wrote my name in places I'd never see.
Spoke devotion into silence.
Loved me in theory
and called it protection.

**This is for the almost that
kept you lonely.**

THE SPILL

You said you always liked me.
Said I was beautiful – even back then.
Said you saw something in me before the shine.
Before the voice.
Before the soft got sharp.

But you never said it when I needed to hear it.

You watched me ache for scraps.
Watched me question my worth in rooms you stood
inside.
And you said nothing.

Because it was easier to love me in silence
than to risk who knows what.

You kept your desire clean.
Polished. Nostalgic.

Untouched by rejection. Unbothered by timing.

And now –
now that I've become
something I can stand inside,
you want to tell me how long you've been
"looking."

But love that won't rise to name you is something
else entirely.
It's fantasy.

It's comfort.
It's a story you told yourself to feel connected
to a version of me you never dared to reach for.

Maybe you thought it was romantic –
to reveal your secret now.
Like it would move me.
Like it would matter.

But all it did was remind me:
you saw me hurting back then,
and kept your mouth full of compliments
you were too preoccupied to give.

That's not tenderness.
That's emotional thrift.
Wanting me at a discount
after I paid full price to become myself.

Keep it.

THE BURIAL

You don't get to want me now.
I needed your courage, not your confession.
Keep the sentiment.
I kept the silence.

THE SURRENDER

She wrote the year –
just the year –
on a torn scrap of cloth.
It was the one where she most needed to be seen.
Then she poured earth over it.
Not her good, fresh soil either.
The dry kind that blows away easy.

She didn't mark it.
Didn't name them.
Didn't cry.

She just placed a rock on top,
big enough to say:

"You were too late. Stay buried."

IT ROSE SLOW.
UNCLEAN.
HALF-WRECKED.
BUT STILL TRUE.
THE HUSH WILL KEEP IT.
IT'S BEEN NAMED.

THE REFUSAL

*Offerings to Every No That Got
Stuck in My Teeth*

I SAID IT ONCE IN MY SPIRIT.
I'M SAYIN' IT OUT LOUD NOW.
THIS IS WHERE I HEXED
INSTEAD OF HEALED.
WHERE I SLAMMED THE DOOR
AND SALTED THE FLOOR.
WHERE I NAMED WHAT
TOUCHED ME WRONG AND SPIT
BEHIND IT.
EVERY PIECE OF GRACE I
SWALLOWED
COMES UP MEAN.
THIS AIN'T PRETTY.
IT'S PAYBACK.
IT'S JUSTICE.

an offering to
the grown man who thought
"hey stranger" was a spell

For the fool who thought absence was lubricant.

They disappeared.
Let the silence get thick.
Then came back, summoning softness,
like they hadn't ghosted a whole garden.

This is for the lazy suitors who confuse neglect with mystery.

THE SPILL

You really typed that shit like that was enough, huh?

"hey stranger"

No punctuation. No apology.
Just those two words –
like they were magic.

Like they could undo your absence.
Unsend the silence.
Resurrect the version of me who didn't know
better.

You thought I'd swoon.
Laugh.
Text back "You're wild" like we were just two
people who lost touch,
and not one person who vanished and one who
survived it.

"Hey stranger" isn't an invitation.
It's an insult.

You skipped the check-in.
Skipped the part where you ask if I'm okay.

Skipped every mile between the last time I heard
from you and the woman I've become since.

And now you're barely in my messages skipping on my last nerve.
I can't even put this sorry shit in the group chat.

You really thought two words could bring me back?

No.
You don't get a second entrance.
Not with lowercase energy.
Not with ghost vibes.
Not with ashy hands that only reach when they're empty.

You mistook nostalgia for permission.
But I outgrew the door you walked through.
And I changed the locks, pookie.

You already made me a stranger.
Don't act surprised that I
chose to stay one.

Blocked.

THE BURIAL

I don't respond to echoes.
I don't return to absence.
I don't chase soft tricks dressed as miracles.

THE SURRENDER

She didn't screenshot it.
Didn't send it to a friend.
Didn't analyze the tone like she used to.

She just stared at the message
for a full ten seconds.
Long enough to feel nothing.
Long enough to remember everything.

Then she blocked the number.
Deleted the thread.
Buried the name in the dirt of her "used to."

No drama. No final words.

Just a silent refusal to play dead for someone who
never knew what to do with the living.

an offering to the mistake i kept repeating because the lesson was cute

For the bad idea I couldn't stop kissing.

I knew better –
but damn if the smile didn't land soft.
It was never love,
just a sweet place to forget who I was.

This is for the ache that came dressed like fun.

THE SPILL

I saw the warning signs.
I read them.
I highlighted them.
Then I folded them into a paper airplane and threw
it straight into his lap.

You weren't confusing.
You were consistent.

Late texts.
Long silences.
That perfect ratio of attention and neglect that
made my intuition shut up just long enough for you
to get through the door.

And baby, when you came through that door?
I forgot everything I promised my therapist.

I knew what this was.
I even joked about it.
"Here I go again!"
Like it was a game. Like I wasn't spiraling.

But you were charming.
You were familiar.

You had a nice smile and good…hands.

You matched the hollow I never dared to name.

The exact shape of the void.

So I let you teach me the same lesson.
Again.
Because this time, I thought maybe I could pass the
class without turning in the assignment.

Spoiler:
I didn't.

I ended up tired, dehydrated, emotionally
overdrafted, and pretending it was growth just
because I didn't cry this time.

You were the kind of mistake I romanticized.
The one I defended.
The one I swore was a cord when it was just a
shared playlist, a flicker of chemistry, and a sprinkle
of delusion.

But I can't even be mad at you.
You told me who you were.
You showed me.
And I winked at the red flag like it was a love note.
Took it between my teeth like a rose –
and danced the dumb bitch tango 'til my feet bled.

You didn't lie to me.

THE BURIAL

I saw the sign.
I ignored it.
I survived it.
May I never be that entertained by harm again.

Let the dirt decide your return.

THE SURRENDER

She gathered every little item that reminded her of
him:
the song, the screenshot, the lace.
Put them in a shoebox.
Taped it shut with duct tape, painter's tape, and
hope.

Wrote "Return to Sender" across the top in red
lipstick.
Then carried it outside like it owed her money.

She dug the hole with her bare hands,
threw the box in,
and dropped one (1) single rose on top.

Not for romance.
For drama.

Then she dusted off her knees,
took a slow sip of iced tea,
and said to the wind:
"That was fun. Never again."

an offering to muthafuckahs who haggled me for my worth

For the ones who were convinced
my value was up for debate.

They loved the glow
but questioned the price.
Wanted the magic –
just not at full cost.

**This is for the fools who
thought you didn't know you
were the altar and the offering.**

THE SPILL

You didn't come to witness.
You came to weigh.

Measured what you could take
against what I didn't yet know I was owed.
And when I named the cost –
you scoffed.
Laughed like it was cute.
Like I was cute.
Said I should be grateful
anybody wanted me at all.

You saw worth.
Real worth.
And still tried to talk me down.

Tried to touch what came from women who prayed
before they ate.
Tried to claim what I pulled from grave-quiet
places.
Tried to own it with compliments, with scarcity,
with smirks.

You didn't offer presence.
You offered proximity –
Like being near you was a form of payment.

And I almost said yes.
Almost handed you the last of what I hadn't named
yet.

58

But I won't lower the price
just because you showed up broke.

Not anymore.

THE BURIAL

I name the full price.

I call back what was taken.
I refuse the half-hand,
the empty gaze,
the almost-love.

What you would not pay,
you will not hold.

Let the dirt decide your return.

THE SURRENDER

The ground was turned by hand –
no tools.
No metal.
Just fingers, calloused and sure,
digging slow like memory.

She laid the scrap of cloth in the hollow –
still stained with what was taken,
still loud with what was owed.

Over it: grave dirt.
A pinch of red clay.
A name written backward in salt.

No fire.
No chant.
Only the weight of the soil
closing in
like it knew exactly who had trespassed.

Nothing was asked.
Only returned.

an offering to the bitch who still wears my skin

For the echo that thinks it's the origin.

She parades in my light like she earned it.
Poses in my past like it's hers to hold.
Wears my voice like stolen silk.
Craves the cadence, not the cost.

This is for the knockoff that forgot it was counterfeit.

THE SPILL

You didn't want my light.
You wanted my shape.
My story.
My scars.
The very breath pattern of my survival.

You studied me like scripture –
but only the verses you thought you could repeat
louder and with better branding.

You tried to move like me,
talk like me,
borrow the weight of my walk
without ever bleeding for it.

But skin doesn't stretch for strangers.
It shrinks.
And every time you stepped inside my rhythm, it
showed.
The performance cracked.
The truth leaked through your seams.
You were a can of biscuits.

Sweetness, I didn't become this by watching.
I became this by *bearing*.

And you –
You dressed in the ashes and thought that made
you burned.
You wanted the shine, not the scorch.

But you don't know how to hold heat like I do.
You don't know what it cost to feel safe inside this
body.

I bled for this self.
Buried versions of me just to keep this one alive.
And you thought you could wear it like costume
jewelry.

You didn't want to honor me.
You wanted to be me.
And not even the best parts –
just the ones that made you feel close to glory
without earning it.

But this isn't envy.
Nah.
This is theft.

And I see you now.
In every sentence that sounds almost like mine.
In every gesture you softened to fit the skin you
couldn't grow.

Return it.
Remove it.
Fester in your own name.

THE BURIAL

I salt this imitation.

I bind the reach.
May your tongue trip every time you try to sound
like me.
May your skin itch
every time you try to fit mine.

THE SURRENDER

She didn't fold anything neatly.
She spit in the dirt, just once,
then wrote her name in the mess – not her own
name. *Hers.*

Took a shred of fabric someone once said looked
like her –
cut it in half.
Not symbolic. Just final.

She placed it in a jar with salt, black pepper, and
crushed eggshell.
Shook it once for the lies.
Twice for the fuckin' nerve.
Three times for every time she bit her tongue.

Then she buried it face-down so the mimicry would
corrupt in reverse.

No apology.
No prayer.
Just this:

"If you ever try me again —
bring a shovel."

an offering to
the apology i withheld to
keep the upper hand

For the silence I weaponized
to feel whole again.

I measured their mercy by the inch.
Spoke in blank stares and half-lidded shrugs.
Let them sweat in my stillness.

**This is for the leverage you
pulled from the pause.**

THE SPILL

I should've said it.
You were owed that much.

Not because you were perfect.
Not because I was entirely wrong.
But because what I withheld was small – and what it
cost was not.

I knew how to make it right.
I had the words.
But I held them like weapons.

Tasted "I'm sorry" on my tongue,
then swallowed it – slow.
Not because it wasn't true,
but because letting it go would've meant tumbling
from the high ground.
The power.
The illusion that I'd been the one done wrong.

It wrapped around me just right.

I liked the way you paused before speaking.
The way your sentences got careful around me.
The way I could feel you reaching –
not for closeness,
but for my approval.

But silence always collects.
And I paid for mine with intimacy.

70

Paid for it with trust.
Paid for it with the version of us that could've
healed if I'd just stepped down first.

Instead, I watched you fold.
Watched you apologize for things you didn't do just
to close the gap between us.

And still –
I held the apology like a crown.
Like a victory I'd earned.
Like a goddamn prize.

But it wasn't a win.
It was a wall.

And I live behind it now.

THE BURIAL

I hurt them on purpose.
Called it truth.
Watched them bleed
and stayed quiet.

That don't need forgiveness.
It needs dirt.

THE SURRENDER

She sat with the words in her mouth,
rolled them around like marbles.
Not heavy – just dangerous if dropped.

Wrote the apology on parchment,
nothing flowery.
Just the line.
The moment.
The admission.

Then she folded it once.
Twice.
And slid it under the leg of the table that always
rocked.

The one that wobbled every time she sat down to
rest.
The one she never fixed.
Now it stands steady.
And she never speaks of it.
But she knows what's holding it up.

an offering to
the scab i picked
just to watch it bleed

For the wounds I turned into weapons.

It was never about healing.
I wanted them to hurt loud.
Wanted proof they were human.
So I dragged the sharp edge across my own
memory just to hear them scream.

**This is for the part of you
that couldn't bear
to bleed alone.**

THE SPILL

I knew where to press.
I always do.

It wasn't instinct.
It was memory.
I remembered the way their eyes dropped when
certain truths got too close.
The breath they held when the air turned sharp.
The silence that wasn't absence – just restraint.

And still,
I asked the question like I was curious.
Like I didn't already know the bruise was still
tender.

It felt like evidence.
Like proof that I hadn't been the only one cut open.

But really?
It was cruelty dressed in connection.

I picked at the fresh skin
because I wanted to see if they still bled.
Because part of me needed them broken to feel
bonded.
Needed them undone so I wasn't the only one
unraveling.

I smiled while I did it.
Said things like "I'm just being honest."

Said "I thought we were past this."
Said "you're still so sensitive."

But I wasn't speaking truth.
I was *twisting* it.

I made them explain pain they hadn't even survived
yet.
Watched them shrink –
and called it transparency.

And when they pulled away,
I acted confused.
Like I hadn't lit the fire.
But I know what I did.
I peeled back their healing just to prove it hadn't
taken.
Not because I cared.
Because I was lonely in my damage.

And it felt good to have company.

THE BURIAL

I won't dress it up.
I won't mourn it.
That moment was mine –
and so was the damage.

It wasn't processing.
It was payback.

It wasn't their wound I reopened.
It was mine –
and I dragged them through it anyway.

THE SURRENDER

She lit nothing.
Didn't cleanse the room.
Didn't bless the silence.

Just sat with her hands flat on her thighs
while the urge clawed at her throat.

She laid the scrap of cloth in the hollow –
still stained with what was taken,
still loud with what was owed.

Over it: grave dirt.
A pinch of red clay.
A name written backward in salt.

No fire.
No chant.
Only the weight of the soil
closing in
like it knew exactly who had trespassed.

Nothing was asked.
Only returned.

You closed the door without ceremony. Just locked it and kept sweeping. The silence was loud, but so were you — for once, only to yourself.

THE CARRYING

Offerings to What My Body Still Remembers

I DIDN'T PACK THIS.
I JUST WOKE UP WITH IT IN MY
MOUTH.
IN MY HIPS.
IN THE SILENCE BETWEEN YES
AND NO.
I CARRIED IT LIKE BREATH.
LIKE PRAYER.
LIKE SOMETHING THAT
WOULDN'T LEAVE UNLESS I DID.
THIS IS THE WEIGHT I NAMED
SURVIVAL.
BUT IT'S BEEN DRAGGING ME ALL
THE SAME.
READ SLOW.
IT'S STILL BLEEDING IN PLACES I
CAN'T REACH.

**an offering to
the red that
didn't mean danger**

For the blood they taught me to fear
instead of revere.

It came without warning –
not like a threat, but like a truth.
And they taught me to hide it.
To pad it, perfume it, pretend it was shame.

**This is for the river you
were told to treat like waste
instead of wonder.**

THE SPILL

They told me to hide it.
To roll it up in scented cotton
and lie about the moon twisting my insides
and never let the red reach the surface –
Even my bleeding knew to behave.

The first time it came,
I didn't cry.
I hid it.
I stole.
I promised God I would never do the whatever it
that caused his wrath again.

I treated the next time like nothing had come
before.

I apologized for the inconvenience.
Said to no one that I'd be more careful next time,
like leaking was a failure.
Like it was my turn to break the unspoken rule.
Like I was marked for trouble.

No one said it was sacred soon enough.
No one called the power by its name.
They just handed me products
and called it hygiene.
Bought me a new skirt and accused me of
womanhood.

So, I treated the blood like shame.

Like something to manage, not meet.
Clenched through cramps beneath fluorescent
lights.
Hid in tiled sanctuaries where the body could speak
wild.
Smiled through clot-thick fatigue.

I tried not to look sick,
even when I was in pain.

No one talked about the
hard pull that came early,
or how it sometimes felt like grief before loss.
No one said that the first whisper from the womb
could feel like betrayal –
like it had gone feral without asking permission.

The women I knew didn't say much.
They'd hand over pads like contraband.
Offer painkillers like favors.
They didn't share stories –
they handed down sayings.
I didn't learn from them that cycles had seasons,
or that my mood was a message.
I just learned how to cover up quicker.
How to keep moving.

So, I didn't ask questions.
Didn't track, didn't tend.
Just braced for the bleed
and wore whatever version of me
hurt the least.

Years passed like that –
bleeding, bracing, pretending not to notice.

And when someone told me
they didn't "believe in" cycles –
I laughed.
Not because it was funny,
but because I'd built a whole life
around denying mine.

That was the day I stopped siding with
the part of myself that found my body inconvenient
and started listening to
what it had been trying to say
the whole time.

THE BURIAL

I name the blood not broken.
I name the clot not cursed.
I name the red holy,
the rhythm mine.

May the dirt carry what was once called shame.

THE SURRENDER

The cloth was soaked but not cleaned.
She folded it into a square
and placed at the base of a tree
no one had named.

A line of salt was poured around the trunk –
not to trap,
but to recognize.

No prayers.
No perfume.
Just the sound of something sacred
being handed back to the earth
without apology.

an offering to
the bite that
made me feel safe

For the hunger I tried to hush with something
that couldn't hold me.

It fed the part of me that didn't speak.
The one that needed to feel full of anything.
I called it care.
But it never stayed long enough to bless me.

**This is for the appetite that
made liars of us both.**

THE SPILL

You were the first thing that didn't tense up when I
needed too much.

You didn't shame me.
Didn't back away.
Didn't ask me to explain the empty spaces – you
just filled it.

You were always there.
At 2am.
After the fight.
During the silence.
Right before the tears.
Right after I swore I'd stop.

You didn't say no.
You said "Here."

And I took it.
Again.
And again.
And again.

Not just the sugar.
Not just the salt.
I swallowed whole moments I never got to feel.
I chewed through loneliness.
I binged through grief.
I ate like I was trying to replace touch with texture.

And when the shame came,
you were still there.

You watched me cry and kept offering more.
You let me lie to myself gently –
"This is comfort."
"This is control."
"This is fine."

But it wasn't.
And you knew that.
You knew I'd trade my body for a moment of
numbness.
Knew I'd gorge on regret and still come back
hungry.

You didn't cause the wound.
But you learned how to keep it open.
You fed it.
You became it.

And I kept calling it sustenance.

THE BURIAL

I unlearn the offering.
I call the hunger by its real name.
I spit out the comfort that came wrapped in silence.

I will not worship what weakens me.

THE SURRENDER

She didn't cleanse.
She didn't detox.
She sat.

an offering to
the ache i never
interrupted

For the pain I thought I had to
earn my way out of.

It didn't just knock.
It moved in.
I let it stay because leaving felt like betrayal.

**This is for the colorless
bruise you babysat
like it was kin.**

THE SPILL

Some pains didn't stop me.
They shaped me.

The throbbing in my knees from standing too long,
in cheap shoes that looked expensive.
The cramp in my wrist from pretending my hand
was always open.
The tightness in my jaw from grinding down every
no I wanted to say out loud.

I didn't rest.
I recalibrated.

Adjusted the limp.
Shifted the bag.
Smiled bigger when it started to throb.
I didn't even call it pain –
just "doing what needed to be done."

I worked while hurting.
Cleaned while hurting.
Sat in silence with people who called me strong,
sturdy even, and didn't notice I was stiff from
overuse.

And the worst part?
I got good at it.
Built a rhythm around it.

Taught others how to push through

instead of how to pause.

The ache didn't break me.
It became a skill.
And for years,
that scared me more than the pain ever did.

THE BURIAL

I return what I bore too long.
I name function not freedom.
I sever usefulness from worth.

May the dirt unteach me.

THE SURRENDER

She placed the shoe in the ground sole-up,
still shaped by the arch of years she didn't pause.

Beside it, she pressed down a snapped pencil
and an unused sick day slip –
creases still sharp,
never signed.
No oil.
No salt.
Just her hands,

packing dirt like she meant it.

She didn't speak.
Not even to herself.
The silence had work to do.

When it was done,
she left the ground smooth.
No marker.
No blessing.
Just a patch of earth
that no longer owed her anything.

an offering to
the tension that
outlived the threat

For the false peace that stiffened my jaw.

The shouting stopped,
but the quiet still made my stomach tighten.
My body kept the pattern,
even after the threat forgot my name.

**This is for the calm that
came too late to
feel like safety.**

THE SPILL

I brace before joy,
like it might vanish if I let my guard down.

My shoulders rise like they're answering a question I
didn't ask.
I scan silence for signs of collapse.
Even kindness makes me check for the edge.

It doesn't take much –
a pause in a sentence,
the wrong tone on a good day,
a door closing just a little too loud.

And my chest tightens,
not from fear,
but from memory.

My body learned the art of readiness
from years of waiting on things that never came
or came too late
or came sharp.

There's no violence in the room.
But my breath still forgets itself.
My jaw still locks.
My ribs still hold air like it might be the last.

I don't panic.
I prepare.
Without warning. Without choice.

Without anyone noticing how much it costs.
And still –
I love this body for that.
For not waiting on proof.
For catching the blow that never landed.
For remembering how to survive
even after I started living.

THE BURIAL

I name stillness safe.
I name silence not a threat.
I name this body not overreacting,
but remembering.

May the dirt carry the alarms I no longer need.

THE SURRENDER

She didn't make a fuss.
No tools.
No salt.
Just a quiet descent into the ground –
palms flat, chest low, head bowed
not in prayer,
but in release.

A steady breath passed through ivory,
then another,
until the rhythm matched the insects nearby.

No words.
Only weight shifting from spine to soil.

Something was laid down in that stillness.
Not banished.
Just returned.

**an offering to
the story i told so i could
stay innocent**

For the rewrite that made it easier to sleep.

I left out the part where I knew better.
Smoothed the edges 'til they couldn't cut me.
Played naive so I wouldn't have to name the
harm...or admit I let it happen.

This is for the lie you needed to feel like a good person.

THE SPILL

There's a version of the story I used to tell.
Clean. Convincing.
All wound, no weapon.
A story where I was the one who got left, not the
one who let the door stay open.
Where I was misread – never manipulative.
Where I was broken – not brittle.
Where I was a victim, not the portal through which
something ancient reached its fresh supply.

I repeated that story because it was mostly true.
But "mostly" is a hell of a drug when you're trying
to stay soft in your own eyes.

I said I didn't know better.
I said I was trying.
I said I never meant to.

But if I'm honest –
there were times I needed someone to feel what I
couldn't name in myself.
Times I provoked pain just to recognize the shape
of my own.

Times I punished the innocent because it was safer
than confronting the ones who hurt me.

That's the part I never said.
Because I wanted to be the wounded one.
The brave one.

The one who crawled out of the mud with grace in
her mouth and swampy water in her lungs.

But I didn't always crawl out.
Sometimes I dragged someone else in with me.
Sometimes I bit back when no one asked for blood.

There's no apology in this.

Just…
a reckoning.

With the part of me that weaponized her own pain.
With the part of me that blamed survival while
knowing better.
With the part of me that wasn't innocent – and
didn't need to be.

That's the truth.
That's the freedom.

I'm not clean.
And I won't bleach the story.

THE BURIAL

I release the lie I told in my own name.
I do not need to be innocent to be worthy.
I do not need to be clean to be free.
I name the harm I collected.
I name the harm I caused.

I carry both – not as guilt, but as proof I'm still learning.
And still here.

THE SURRENDER

She cracked her knuckles before she touched the paper.
Wrote like she was testifying – not confessing.

No poetry.

No flourishes.
Just the moment it turned,
and what she turned into.
She folded it fast.
Like she didn't want to see the words once they were real.
Wrapped it in the hem
of an old shirt she used to love,
and tied it shut with thread pulled from her own hairbrush.

Buried it shallow.
Not to forget.
But so the earth could watch it decompose.

Then she pressed her palm flat to the mound and
said nothing.
Didn't hum.
Didn't pray.

She just listened.
To what left her.
To what stayed.

**an offering to
college**

For the institution that sold me arrival but made me prove I belonged.

I showed up ready to bloom –
and got graded on how quiet I could be.
Gave them everything but my blood
and still left without a piece of paper.

This is for the debt you carry that's too long for a ledger.

THE SPILL

I was supposed to be finding myself.
But mostly I just lost sleep, lost time,
and learned how to perform whatever version of
me survived the semester.

I drank things I didn't like with people I didn't trust
to avoid silence.
I let the wrong hands touch me
because I thought being chosen –
even badly – was better than being invisible.

I smiled in places where I felt invisible anyway.

I called it freedom,
but I was just unwatched.
There's a difference.

And I did learn the things.
But not in the classroom.
I learned how to swallow my voice in group
projects.
How to twist my tone so that professors would take
me seriously.

How to laugh at jokes that weren't funny
so I wouldn't be the angry one.
The sensitive one.
The "Super Black" who always had something to
say.

I wrote essays about systems that were breaking me,
and got A's for how well I understood them.
Told myself that was strength.
That this is what pushing through looked like.

But honestly?
I don't remember too much more of it.

I remember the contortion.
The performance.
The version of me who tried so hard to sound
smart enough, chill enough, good enough to make it
out with a future.

And I did make it out.
Not with a cap and gown.
But with stories that earned me more than credit
hours.

I got two classes away from finishing.
And still –
they'll never know how much I carried just to sit in
those rooms.

I'm not ungrateful.
But I'm not going to romanticize it either.

Some of the most beautiful, brutal years of my life
ended like a spell left open –
no closure,
no weighted paper with embossed words,
just a ghost where my name should've been.

THE BURIAL

I don't need a ceremony to be complete.
I don't need a paper to make me credible.
I was enough the whole damn time.
And I still am.

THE SURRENDER

She pulled out the syllabus from her last class.
The one she never got to finish.
She didn't read it.
Just folded it slow – like a receipt from something
she paid too much for.

She added her student ID,
the dead highlighter,
a notebook full of pristine notes for the test she
didn't take.

Then she found the email.
The one that marked the end of it all –
not with a celebration,
but with a quiet stop.

She buried them together.
No applause.
No regrets.

Just her hand in the dirt and the truth in her chest.

"I did the work.
Whether they recognize it or not –
I made it out with my mind."

SOME OF IT WAS NEVER YOURS
TO CARRY. SOME OF IT CLUNG
ANYWAY. THAT'S HOW IT WORKS.

THAT'S WHY IT'S SO HEAVY.

THE LOWERING

Offerings to What I Had to Bury
Without Witness

I AIN'T HERE TO SAY MUCH.
JUST TO COVER WHAT AIN'T BEEN
COVERED.
SOME THINGS GOT LEFT TOO
LONG IN THE OPEN.
BUZZIN'. BRUISIN'.
DRAWIN' FLIES AND WHISPERS.
SO I BROUGHT 'EM HERE.
NO STONE. NO PREACHER.
JUST DIRT.
AND THE HUSH IT KNOWS HOW
TO KEEP.
DON'T SAY SORRY.
DON'T SAY NOTHIN'.
JUST HELP ME COVER IT RIGHT
'FORE THE NIGHT FINDS IT
AGAIN.

an offering to
the dream that refused
to die clean

For the thing I tried to let go,
but it bled all over me anyway.

It was buried without a eulogy,
and it kept breathing through the soil.
Showed up in my sleep,
to ask if I meant it.

**This is for what you outgrew
but never unloved.**

THE SPILL

You were supposed to be buried.
Not dragged into every new version of me.

But there you were.
In every almost.
Every detour.
Every quiet moment where I let my guard down
and you curled up beside me like you still had a
place.

You were beautiful.
Don't get me wrong.
You were mine –
until you weren't.

I outgrew you.
Or maybe I just outlived you.
But you never let go.

You kept visiting,
disguised as "what if,"
as "maybe still,"
as "try one more time."

You weren't just a dream.
You were a goddamn haunting.

And I didn't fight it at first.
I let you hang around.
Let you sit on my chest at night

like a story I hadn't finished telling.

But every time I tried to build a new life,
you knocked from underneath the floorboards.

And I'm tired.
Tired of making room for what can't feed me.
Tired of calling your ghost hope.

You could've died clean.
You didn't.

And now I have to do what you wouldn't.

THE BURIAL

I name you cherished.
I name you done.
I name you dead – and not coming back.
May the dirt keep you better than I did.

THE SURRENDER

She didn't cry.

Just pressed the folded page
into the center of the garden,
where nothing ever took root right.

No flowers.
No herbs.
Just this –
a quiet plot for a dream that wouldn't stay gone.

She placed a flat stone over it,
carved nothing into it.

an offering to
the question i should've
asked at the table

For the silence I dressed up as respect.

I passed the peas and swallowed the truth.
Let the room stay whole
so that I could stay invited.
But that question still hums in my bones –
louder than the comfort I tried to create.

**This is for what you didn't
say because you knew
they couldn't hold it.**

THE SPILL

The table was set,
but the silence was older than the meal.

I could've asked.
Could've said, "Why didn't you stop it?"
Or, "Do you really not remember?"
Or just, "Was it worth it?"

But I passed the rice.
Laughed at a joke I didn't think was funny.
Swallowed the hurt like it was seasoned just right.

Every time someone reached across me,
it felt like history smacking me in the mouth.
And I stayed quiet,
because the roast was tender,
and the elders were tired,
and someone said grace like that made it clean.

I had the words.
I just didn't have the permission.

So I carried that question through every holiday,
let it stink behind my teeth,
and watched them go to their graves
thinking they got away with it.

They didn't.
But I still didn't ask.

THE BURIAL

I name what I never spoke.
I name the plate clean, but the truth raw.
I name my silence not peace.

May the dirt take the words that burned through my
tongue.

THE SURRENDER

She laid the fork in the soil like a weapon turned in.
Laid the napkin like a shroud.

She didn't light a candle.
Just poured water over the spot
until the ground could taste what she couldn't say.

There was no chair left for her there.
And no appetite, either.

Just a patch of dirt
where questions went to starve.

an offering to
the exit i rehearsed
but never made

For the doors I never walked through –
even when I wanted to.

I whispered my leave like a prayer,
Folded my longing into silent routines.
Practiced my freedom in secret.
But stayed anyway.

**This is for the moment you
almost chose yourself...
and didn't.**

THE SPILL

I said it all
but only in my head.
Left a hundred times.
None of them out loud.
Stood in showers and walked down hallways
practicing silence like it was armor.

I imagined the slam of the car door,
the stillness afterward.
Practiced my lines in the mirror until they stopped
sounding like me.

I didn't stay because I didn't know it was wrong.
I stayed because I couldn't figure out how to leave
right.

Somewhere along the way, the goodbye became
part of the fantasy.
Not just the exit,
but the way I'd be understood on my way out.
I wanted them to hear it all and get it.
I wanted closure and clarity and maybe even care.

But you can't script someone else's listening.

So, I chewed the words.
And then swallowed the shards.

And then digested the version of me that still
wanted to speak.

THE BURIAL

No more dress rehearsals.
No more imaginary exits.

I will not keep living inside stories I never got to
tell.

This time, I'm leaving – not the room, not the
person.
But the need to make the leaving beautiful.

I will not wait for the perfect goodbye.
I will not grieve what never unfolded.

I am allowed to walk away with nothing but breath
in my chest
and the sound of my own feet, finally moving.

THE SURRENDER

She didn't walk out.

She kneeled.

One hand to the ground.
The other still clenched.

She pressed something into the dirt.
Not hurried. Not harsh. Just steady.
She dug a small hole with her palm.
Lined it with bigger silence.
She placed it there –
that unseen thing –
and covered it with earth.

No words.

Only the sound of breath loosening.
Only the hush of dirt receiving.
She wiped her hands on her thighs.
Stood.
Turned.
And left the ground to remember what she didn't
say.

an offering to
the year i can't
remember on purpose

For the season I erased to survive.

There are memories I don't misplace –
I exile them.
Buried deep in overwork, new lovers,
and stories that sound less like screaming.

This is for what you refuse to remember because the naming might undo you.

THE SPILL

You don't get a scrapbook.
You don't get poems.
You don't get a damn thing from me.

Because I know what happened that year.
Even if I don't keep the details.
Even if I let the months run together
like a blur I never wanted to sharpen.

I know what I felt waking up.
The heaviness.
The choke of routine.
The stretch of pretending I was okay
long after I'd stopped trying to be.

You were survival mode.
You were numbness with a name.
You were me,
half-dead in a life that still demanded performance.

And yes, I made it out.
But I didn't carry you with me.

I left you behind on purpose.
Like a locked room with no windows.
Like a diary I burned before reading it back.
Don't ask me what songs I liked.
What I wore.
What I celebrated.

I was breathing.
That's it.

You don't get a story.
You get a grave.

THE BURIAL

I name you survived.
I name you hollow.
I name you finished.
May the dirt erase your shape without apology.

THE SURRENDER

She didn't bring flowers.

Just a strip of calendar paper,
weather-stained and torn,
with no writing on it.

She folded it once,
twice,
then pressed it into the mud
like she was sealing something shut.

She didn't whisper.

Didn't mark the spot.

She just stood there long enough
to be sure the silence would hold.

Then turned her back
and let the year die
without turning into memory.

**an offering to
the final goodbye
i forfeited**

For the ending I didn't attend but still grieve.

I stayed away as if it would hurt less.
Tried not to picture the casket.
Told myself distance was dignity.
But the silence buried me too.

**This is for the farewell that
never got to happen –
and never stopped echoing.**

THE SPILL

I didn't go.

And I've rewritten that sentence in my head a
hundred ways —
so it would sound less selfish,
less hollow,
less like abandonment in a suit.

But the truth is simple:
I didn't go.

Not because I didn't care.
Because I cared too much to be seen falling apart.
Because I feared what would surface.
Because I didn't know how to mourn someone who
never got to become.

You were my little brother.
And I missed your funeral.

I missed the poems. The stories. The badly folded
programs with your face too close to the edge of
the photo.

I missed the air inside the church.
The shared agony.
The closed casket.
The hug I might've needed to collapse into.

THE BURIAL

I didn't say goodbye.
But I never stopped holding you.
And I let the silence say what I couldn't carry to the room.

THE SURRENDER

She didn't wear black.

She lit nothing. Burned nothing.
She just sat with the picture.
The one that never made it into a frame —still curled at the edges, still breathing youth.

She placed it on the bare earth.
No altar. No prayer.

Just soil and memory.
Wind and regret.
She said his name once.
Not to the sky. Not to the trees.
Just to the dirt —the only thing still steady enough to hold it.

And she stayed there.
Not for closure.

Not for healing.
Just long enough to stop rehearsing the goodbye
and let it happen –
as she was, not as she should've been.

an offering to the lie that kept me warm

For the kind of comfort that costs too much.

It curled up beside me like a pet
I didn't name.
Kept it fed just enough to stay.
Didn't ask for the truth…just obedience.
This won't leave gently.

This is for the loyalty you gave to your own undoing.

THE SPILL

You were never true.
Not even close.
But damn, you were comfortable.

I let you curl around me in the cold.
Let you hum in my ear when the truth got too
sharp.
Let you stay –
because believing you cost less than surviving
without you.

You told me they cared.
That I wasn't alone.
That they didn't mean it.
That I could fix it.
That I just needed to wait, be better, love harder,
speak softer, pray more, want less.

You told me I was safe
when I wasn't.

And I believed you –
because I needed something to believe in.

You didn't protect me.
You just paused the breaking.

And I held you like gospel.

Even when the facts started clawing at the door.

Even when I knew better.
Even when the silence turned to static
and I could barely hear myself think without your
voice in the way.

You didn't love me.
You lulled me.

And now I must let you go –
sever you without further injuring the part of me
that needed you.

THE BURIAL

I name you a mercy I couldn't afford.
I name your comfort counterfeit.
I name myself forgiven for needing you.

May the dirt dissolve your shape
before I ever reach for it again.

THE SURRENDER

She laid the ribbon down.
The one she used to tie every excuse together.

Took the photo frame,
flipped it face-down in the soil –
glass cracked from when she dropped it,
but never replaced it.

She scattered a small handful of sugar.
Not to sweeten,
but to mark where sweetness once fooled her.

Then she turned the earth slowly,
like burying a pet
she once called by name
but didn't recognize anymore.

YOU CARRIED IT LONGER THAN
THEY KNEW. GRIEVED IT BEFORE
IT EVEN ENDED. SAID GOODBYE
WITHOUT A SCENE. THAT
COUNTS, TOO.

WHAT THE DIRT MADE OF IT

MADE OF IT

*Final Words to Whatever
Survived Me*

I DIDN'T TEND IT.
I DIDN'T WATER IT.
I WASN'T TRYING TO GROW
NOTHIN'.
I JUST LEFT THE PIECES WHERE
THEY FELL.
WALKED OFF BEFORE THE WIND
COULD NAME 'EM.
BUT THE DIRT GOT ITS OWN
MIND.
TOOK WHAT I DROPPED AND
WHISPERED OVER IT. TURNED IT
SLOW.
DIDN'T ASK ME IF I WAS READY.
NOW SOMETHING'S MOVING
UNDER THERE.
I DON'T KNOW IF IT'S MINE.
I DON'T KNOW IF IT'S DONE.

BUT IT ROSE ANYWAY.
SO, I'LL LET IT.

an offering to
the sprout i almost
stepped on

I didn't mean to grow it.
Didn't ask for anything new.
But there it was – small, stubborn, green.
Proof that something tried anyway.

This is... for it.

THE SPILL

(I won't say this loud.
I'll just press it here –
like seed.)

There was something
that kept going
without me.

Something.
Small, and unbothered by my forgetting.

It came up
through all the heaviness I never cleared.
All the grief I let settle like mulch.

Didn't ask for light.
Didn't need direction.
Just found a crack,
and made room.

I almost missed it.
Almost crushed it
while looking for something prettier.

But it rose anyway.

Not for me.
Just because it could.
And now that I've seen it –
I won't pretend it's not there.

The Burial

The ground has done a new thing.
I don't name it.
I don't own it.
I just make room.

The Surrender

She didn't touch it.
Didn't water.
Didn't bless.
Didn't stare.

Just noticed.
And stepped aside.
And let it keep going.

Let them call it bitter.
Let them say you stayed in the dirt too long.
Let them say it should've smelled like forgiveness by
now.

They weren't built to bloom here.
You were.

You buried the lies.
You named the ghosts.
You spat the prayers in tongues only you could
speak.

Now watch what grows from that.

Untamed.
Unruly.
Bright like it's breaking a rule.

Bring the wildflowers anyway.

THE AFTERCARE: A TENDING SPACE FOR THE ONES WHO STAYED

The work is sacred. So is the recovery.

You made it through the dirt.

Through the dragging. The digging. The naming.

Through the spit, the silence, the severance, the surrender.
Maybe you came out sobbing. Maybe you came out silent.
Maybe you're not sure how or if you came out at all.

That's what this part is for.

Aftercare is not about fixing what cracked.
It's about holding what surfaced.
It's about honoring the nervous system that didn't have room to fold – or did – and showed up anyway.

This isn't a workbook.
There are no steps.
Just offerings.

Each entry is here for a different kind of aftermath
–
the fury that won't fade,
the numbness that lingered too long,
the sacred hush you don't want to disturb.
Don't rush.
Don't read it all at once.

Don't try to make this tidy.

Start where you are.
Follow what pulls.
And remember:

You don't have to understand what moved you to
deserve recovery from it.

The work was holy.
But so is the way you stay.

MORE READS FOR YOUR RELEASE

While no book can fix everything, these reads might just offer a spark of insight or a moment of 'aha!' to help you along the way. Remember, it's not about the book itself, but what you do with the tools you find within it!

1. *"The Body Keeps the Score"* by Bessel van der Kolk – This book is great for understanding how trauma is stored in the body and ways to heal through mind-body practices.

2. *"Rising Strong"* by Brené Brown – Perfect for anyone looking to transform their struggles into strength, Brené walks you through the process of rising after a fall.

3. *"It Didn't Start with You"* by Mark Wolynn – This is a powerful read for understanding inherited family trauma and breaking the cycle.

4. *"Radical Acceptance"* by Tara Brach – This book is wonderful for learning how to embrace yourself with compassion and mindfulness.

5. *"The Artist's Way"* by Julia Cameron – Great for anyone looking to reconnect with their creativity and use it as a healing tool.

6. ***"Waking the Tiger"*** by Peter A. Levine –
   This one explores trauma from a somatic
   perspective and offers ways to release it
   from the body.

7. ***"Untamed"*** by Glennon Doyle – A
   powerful and inspiring read about living
   authentically and embracing your true self.

Scan the QR code with your phone to explore these
titles and the growing list of recommended texts.

BURY IT IN THE MUSIC

Here are 13 soundscapes for those who know music isn't background, it's balm.

1. If You Want to Burn Something Down, listen to **Holy Rage, No Apologies.**

   Not all healing sounds like a hymn. Some of it kicks the door off the hinges and sets fire to the porch. This playlist is for righteous rage, the kind you didn't apologize for this time.

2. If You're Ready to Rest Now, listen to **The Soil Is Still Holding You.**

   You don't have to earn your retreat. You don't have to be fixed to be worthy of stillness. This playlist is for laying down the ache, the armor, and the need to be understood.

3. If You Want to Be Touched (But Not by People), listen to **Touched by Earth, Not Hands.**

   This one's for the skin that misses sensation but doesn't want to be reached for. These songs touch you like air, like water, like breath on the back of your neck.

4. If You Want to be Seen but No One's Around, listen to **Witness Me Anyway.**

You laid it bare. Then came the silence.
This playlist is not applause. It's presence.

5. If You're Thinking About Going Back
    (Even When You Know Better), listen to **I
    Know What It Cost Me.**

    Some goodbyes echo sweet. Some come
    back wearing memory like perfume. These
    are songs for the moment you almost called
    and didn't.

6. If You Remembered Something You
    Weren't Ready To, listen to **Memory Is
    Not the Enemy.**

    This playlist wasn't curated to make you
    forget. It's here to sit beside what surfaced,
    without demanding a resolution.

7. If You're Afraid Nothing Will Change,
    listen to **The Ground Is Moving, Even If
    I Can't Feel It Yet.**

    Healing doesn't always roar. Sometimes it
    trembles underground, slow and unseen.
    These songs hum beneath the surface. So
    do you.

8. If You Feel Tender but Unsure What to
    Do with It, listen to **Handle with Care.**

    You're not fragile. You're freshly
    uncovered. Let these songs be silk on the
    parts of you that still feel new.

9. If You Feel Peaceful, But Suspicious About It, listen to **Soft, But Not Stupid.**

   When you've been lied to by peace before, softness can feel like a scam. These songs don't beg you to relax, they show you how it feels to stay.

10. If You Feel Lonely in the Wake of It All, listen to **Echoes Don't Mean You're Alone.**

    You're not echoing into nothing. You're just the only one awake right now. Let these songs keep you company without speaking over the quiet.

11. If You Feel Like You Were Too Much While Reading This, listen to **I Was Never Too Much. Just Too Honest.**

    Maybe they couldn't hold your volume. Your pain. Your honesty. That doesn't mean you were too much. These songs say it louder.

12. If You Want to Undo the Reading, listen to **I Want My Innocence Back.**

    You didn't mean to go this deep. This is for the ones who read something they weren't ready for and stayed anyway.

13. For All of You, listen to **Build Me Up, Don't Bury Me.**

You made it through. Not because you fixed it, but because you stayed. These songs are not a celebration. They're scaffolding.

You can find these playlists and more *Aftercare* by scanning the QR code with your phone.

SOFT INVITATIONS + GENTLE NUDGES

Dirt Still Moving?

If you're not done yet –
if the writing won't let go –
there's more waiting for you.

Unearthed: 13 Prompts the Dirt Kept Quiet
A companion to this book.
Written for the aftermath.
Made for *Aftercare.*
You can also find it here:

letthedirthaveit.latetrao.com

Keep writing.
The dirt knows what it's doing.

Words Keep Coming?

If something in you is still stirring
and hasn't quieted yet, if you found a truth in these
pages that surprised you, you can tell me about it.

Not for fixing.
Not for feedback.
Just for witnessing.

You can send your words, your reflections, or what
the dirt unearthed by visiting the *Aftercare* Portal at:

letthedirthaveit.latetrao.com

This isn't a newsletter.
It's a quiet shelf.
And every story placed on it is held with care.

THE INDEX: A TOOL TO GET WHERE YOU WANNA BE A LITTLE QUICKER

You are holding a grimoire.

Grimoire *(n.)*

A sacred record of spells, rituals, truths, and remembered power.
Historically used to house magical instructions, a grimoire is more than a book; it is a container of knowing, a manual for the unseen, a whispered archive of what has been survived and transmuted.

In your hands, this grimoire does not speak in Latin or list herbs. It speaks in lived experience, in naming, in the grime you dared to touch.
It teaches not how to cast spells but how to release the voice that was damned you to silence.

SOMETHING LIKE A LEGEND

For the Ones Who Like Order, Explanation, and a Little Light on the Path

This grimoire speaks in three tongues:
one that spills,
one that covers,
one that surrenders.

They show up in every **Offering.**
Not to guide you, but to mark what kind of work is being done.

The Spill is what leaked out when holding it in got too heavy.
It's the rupture. The memory. The voice that came back sharp or shaking.
It doesn't ask for permission. It just pours.

The Burial is not healing.
It's the laying-down. The standing up. The nerve.
It's what you say to the dirt when no one else believes you. When living ears could care less.
It's words you say before you cover what's been covering you.

The Surrender is never for show.
It is private work, witnessed in shadow.
A closing gesture. A small defiance. A sacred nothing.
It doesn't invite imitation – only respect.

You don't need to read them in order.
You don't need to understand them all at once.

Let your body recognize what your mind can't name yet.
Let the rhythm show you what kind of truth is moving.
Some pages will spit.
Some will sting.
Some will just sit beside your grief until you're ready to bury it right.
That's the legend.

Now let the dirt speak.

FIND YOURSELF IN THE AFTERMATH

An Index of Return for the Body, the Mind, and the Spirit

You made it to the end, or perhaps you landed here before the last page.

Either way, if you're feeling cracked open, hollow, burning, or undone…
this is your soft way back.

Below is a list of what you might be feeling – and the Offering that knows that feeling well.
Let this index guide you toward the part of the dirt that speaks your language.

If you are haunted by what should have been said...

→ AN OFFERING TO THE QUESTION I SHOULD'VE ASKED AT THE TABLE
→ AN OFFERING TO THE APOLOGY I WITHHELD TO KEEP THE UPPER HAND

If you can't stop revisiting what you never got to leave...

→ AN OFFERING TO THE EXIT I REHEARSED BUT NEVER MADE
→ AN OFFERING TO THE SCAB I PICKED JUST TO WATCH IT BLEED

→ AN OFFERING TO THE TENSION THAT
OUTLIVED THE THREAT
→ AN OFFERING TO THE BITE THAT
MADE ME FEEL SAFE

**If you dressed your wounds in red and called it
warmth...**

→ AN OFFERING TO THE RED THAT
DIDN'T MEAN DANGER
→ AN OFFERING TO THE LIE THAT KEPT
ME WARM

**If you outgrew what you thought would save
you...**

→ AN OFFERING TO COLLEGE
→ AN OFFERING TO THE DREAM THAT
REFUSED TO DIE CLEAN
→ AN OFFERING TO THE MISTAKE I KEPT
REPEATING BECAUSE THE LESSON WAS
CUTE

If your no came too late, or not at all...

→ AN OFFERING TO MUTHAFUCKAHS
WHO HAGGLED ME FOR MY WORTH
→ AN OFFERING TO THE GROWN MAN
WHO THOUGHT "HEY STRANGER" WAS A
SPELL

And if you ever almost gave up on soft things...

→ AN OFFERING TO THE SPROUT I
ALMOST STEPPED ON

→ AN OFFERING TO THE FINAL
GOODBYE I FORFEITED

If you keep forgetting on purpose...

→ AN OFFERING TO THE YEAR I CAN'T
REMEMBER ON PURPOSE
→ AN OFFERING TO THE STORY I TOLD
SO I COULD STAY INNOCENT

If you held it longer than you had to...

→ AN OFFERING TO THE ACHE I NEVER
INTERRUPTED

A BACKWOODS GRIMOIRE
BLESSING: *GO ON THEN*

I ain't gonna say rest easy.
Some things don't rest.
They settle.
They sour.
They sprout.

But if you laid it down honest?
The dirt already took it.

Don't go scratchin' at it later
lookin' for signs or softness.

Some wounds weren't meant to scab.
Some names weren't meant to be kept.
So, if your hands still itch?
Wash 'em in creek water.
Salt 'em.
Leave an egg at the crossroads
and go on.

Not perfect.
Not fixed.
Just not draggin' it no more.

You made it to the bottom.
Ain't nothin' holy 'bout being buried alive
when you were meant to be the one planting.

Go on then.

And don't look back

unless it's to nod
at how far down you went
before you rose.

ACKNOWLEDGMENTS

To the ones who never needed the whole story to
believe me –
Thank you.

To the ones who stayed while I unraveled, re-
buried, came back with new dirt under my nails –

You didn't ask me to be clean. Just true.
You don't know what that costs,
but you paid it anyway.

To every hand that held space for the mess,
the rage,
the tenderness beneath the wreckage,
this book carries your fingerprints in its spine.

To the ancestors who wouldn't let me forget.
To the body that remembered.
To the ghost I finally stopped making small for the
comfort of others –
This is for you.

And to me –
who wrote through the rot,
who told the truth out loud,
who let it rise before it was pretty:

I'm proud of you.
And I'm not surprised.

ABOUT THE AUTHOR

la tetra o. is a writer and ethnopoetic curator.

She gathers stories of grief, ritual, and release –
tracing what was never given language, what lives in
the body, and what echoes across bloodlines.
Her work listens closely to what has been carried,
hushed, or survived.
She writes as both witness and weaver – a steward
of story, lineage, and sacred silence.

connect: @iamlatetrao

If something about the format (not the feeling) interrupted the quality of your reading experience (a misprint, a floating character, or a page out of place), you can let me know at:

books@latetrao.com

Thank you for helping me tend the quality of what was meant to arrive whole.

Disclaimer: This book contains emotionally evocative content, including language that may resemble spells, rituals, or spiritual instructions. These writings are intended as creative, poetic expressions and should not be interpreted as prescriptive or instructional.

The author and publisher are not liable for any outcomes, physical or otherwise, resulting from engagement with this content. Readers are responsible for their own discretion, spiritual safety, and decisions.

ash + anthology

What the fire didn't take, we tell.

Published by Ash + Anthology | © 2025 la tetra o.